Curt Landry

with Paul and Megann Marcarelli

Forward by Perry Stone

The King's Oil

Breaking the Yoke

EXODUS 30
HOLY ANOINTING OIL

D1563294

CURT LANDRY
MINISTRIES

The King's Oil: Breaking the Yoke

by Curt Landry with Paul and Megann Marcellino

Copyright © 2014

First edition

Published and distributed by My Olive Tree

PO Box 193, Fairland, OK 74343

www.MyOliveTree.com

1.800.334.3132

International Standard Book Number: 978-0-9897202-0-5

E-book ISBN: 978-0-9897202-1-2

Layout and Design: Rochelle Hershberger

This book is dedicated to
Dr. TL Osborn,
a man of God who not only taught,
but demonstrated the power of
breaking the yoke
throughout the world.

Dr. TL Osborn and Curt Landry (2012)

Table of Contents

FORWARD

by Perry Stone

We are told in James 5 that if a believer is sick, we are to *"anoint them with oil in the name of the Lord"* (James 5:14-15). We assume this is just normal olive oil which was common in the Mediterranean in that day.

When a Jewish Rabbi and believer, and his son-in-law (a Jewish chemist) received the insight to mix the compounds of Scripture with pure olive oil, some suggest this is wrong—that the oil was for priests. Notice what the Bible teaches about believers: *"And hath made us kings and priests unto God and his Father; to him be glory and dominion for ever and ever"* (Revelation 1:6).

Under the Old Covenant no common person could slay a sacrifice, sprinkle blood on the altar, enter the Holy place to offer incense, light the Menorah, or be anointed with the oil. However, as a kingdom of priests we now offer our sacrifices of praise (Heb. 13:15), we are able to apply the blood of Christ through our confession (Rev. 12:11), and enter the presence of God through the words of our prayer. The incense on the golden altar represented our prayers going up to God (Psalms 141:2).

It is our spiritual position as priests unto God that enables a Jewish believer to prepare this oil and have other believers use it for the purpose of anointing a person! The actual anointing of the Spirit abides in us now (I John 2:27). Under the Old Covenant, only a priest could enter certain areas of the Temple. Today our bodies are the Temple of the Holy Spirit (I Cor. 3:16).

There is a restitution of all things predicted prior to the return of the Lord (Acts 3:21). We have witnessed the restoration of Israel, Jerusalem as the capital, and the return of the Jews from the nations.

According to Isaiah 10:27…May every yoke be broken because of the anointing oil in Yeshua's Name!

Perry Stone

PERRY STONE
MINISTRIES
VOICE OF EVANGELISM/OCI

www.voe.org

"Moreover the LORD spoke to Moses, saying: 'Also take for yourself quality spices—five hundred shekels of liquid myrrh, half as much sweet-smelling cinnamon (two hundred and fifty shekels), two hundred and fifty shekels of sweet-smelling cane, five hundred shekels of cassia, according to the shekel of the sanctuary, and a hin of olive oil. And you shall make from these a holy anointing oil, an ointment compounded according to the art of the perfumer. It shall be a holy anointing oil. With it you shall anoint the tabernacle of meeting and the ark of the Testimony; the table and all its utensils, the lampstand and its utensils, and the altar of incense; the altar of burnt offering with all its utensils, and the laver and its base. You shall consecrate them, that they may be most holy; whatever touches them must be holy. And you shall anoint Aaron and his sons, and consecrate them, that they may minister to Me as priests.

"And you shall speak to the children of Israel, saying: 'This shall be a holy anointing oil to Me throughout your generations. It shall not be poured on man's flesh; nor shall you make any other like it, according to its composition. It is holy, and it shall be holy to you. Whoever compounds any like it, or whoever puts any of it on an outsider, shall be cut off from his people.'"

—Exodus 30:22-33

INTRODUCTION
The King's Oil—A Kingdom of Priests!

The testimony of the restoration of *The King's Oil* is something that is very important for the Church to hear and understand; it speaks of the times and seasons, and is part of the restitution of all things spoken of in Acts 3:19-21:

*"Repent therefore and be converted, that your sins may be blotted out, **so that times of refreshing may come from the presence of the Lord,** and that He may send Jesus Christ, who was preached to you before, whom heaven must receive **until the times of restoration of all things,** which God has spoken by the mouth of all His holy prophets since the world began..."* (Emphasis added)

This generation has the incredible honor of witnessing the restoration of Israel and Jerusalem, and the prophetic return of her people. We have also seen the restoration power of Christians returning to the Jewish roots of their faith. As the Church is truly reuniting with her heritage, we believe that God has unlocked the mystery of *The King's Oil* as a spiritual tool—a symbolic part of the refreshing that the Lord is washing over His Bride, the Church.

The Lord is setting apart His remnant. He is raising up His Bride and preparing us for a great outpouring and awakening. He is equipping us to serve and to become holy vessels of deliverance—and He is breaking the yokes and bondage so that we can serve Him as a Kingdom of Priests!

*"It shall come to pass in that day that his burden will be taken away from your shoulder, and his yoke from your neck, and **the yoke will be destroyed because of the anointing oil**."*
—Isaiah 10:27 (Emphasis added)

Part I

PART I

What is *The King's Oil?*

The King's Oil is holy anointing oil made according to the oil described in Exodus 30.

Originally, the holy anointing oil (Hebrew: *shemen* "oil," *ha-mishchah* "of anointing") was used to consecrate the articles of the Tabernacle, the Temple in Jerusalem, and, of course, the priesthood and kings. It states in Exodus 30 that this anointing oil separated the person or object as being *"most holy"* (Hebrew: *qodesh*) unto the Lord and prepared for service.

Today, *The King's Oil* is produced exclusively by *My Olive Tree* and has been co-sponsored by Curt Landry, Perry Stone, and Ron Phillips. This holy anointing oil has been assembled using ancient apothecary methods—containing a unique aroma, texture, and color exclusive to its Biblical root compounds.

The olive oil that is used in *The King's Oil* is pressed from olives harvested from trees that have been adopted by Believers for the purpose of the restoration of this holy anointing oil. These trees were adopted in Israel through Perry Stone's ministry, *Voice of Evangelism*, and administrated through *My Olive Tree*. We believe that this is a very significant step in the process of producing *The King's Oil*. As Believers, we are authorized to adopt these olive trees, and possess the right to call these trees holy all the way from their roots to their branches laden with olives. Therefore, the olive oil from these trees has been sanctified, and is being used for a purpose most holy unto the Lord.

What Makes *The King's Oil* so Unique?

The physical aspects of *The King's Oil* are unmistakable. Due to the high concentration of spices held within the mixture, the color is quite distinct from the golden olive oil we commonly see in anointing oils. Not all of the spices used in the mixture are soluble in their pure form. As a result, *The King's Oil* has a gritty texture, similar to an ointment—a very tangible anointing.

One can only imagine that if you were to use a large amount of the oil and pour it out over someone's head, or apply a handful of it to an item such as the menorah in the Temple, that there would be little room to mistake the fact that this person, or item, had been touched and anointed with this holy anointing oil made according to Exodus 30. It would be identifiably obvious to all that the person, or item, had been purposely set apart.

— ◆ —

"It is like the precious oil upon the head, running down the beard, the beard of Aaron, running down on the edge of his garments."

—Psalm 133:2

— ◆ —

Can you picture this oil running down the beard and the garment of Aaron? (See Ps. 133:2.) It would have been messy but recognizable; it would have left a lasting impression. We can only assume that Aaron smelled like the anointing for days after—a constant reminder of his priesthood.

The fragrance of *The King's Oil* is very unique, because two of the spices are actually types and forms of cinnamon. There are also hints of other spices such as myrrh. It is hard to comprehend with a small bottle in hand that the Exodus 30 recipe would have made tens of gallons of the final product! With such a massive quantity, the fragrance of the holy anointing oil would have filled the entire Temple as the oil was being produced.

This oil was made and in constant use in the Temple, and the aroma would have remained in the air—a continual reminder of both the sacrifices that were taking place and the holiness that was present. The fragrance of the anointing oil would have been absorbed into the very pores of all that surrounded it.

The King's Oil is believed to be an authentic representation of the oil found in Exodus 30; its use meant to draw the Church closer to her Jewish heritage. As God restores to us aspects of our heritage that were lost in the 3rd century at the Synod of Elvira and the First Council of Nicaea, *The King's Oil* represents just one of the many mysteries that God is unlocking for His Church.

Kings and Priests

This spiritual significance goes beyond the many unique physical attributes *The King's Oil* holds. In the most basic sense, the anointing oil can be used when praying for others, or for anointing your home in the same manner the priests would have anointed items in the Tabernacle. This anointing process was a sign of sanctification or of setting something apart for God's intended use and purpose. It is a tool to destroy the yoke.

The King's Oil represents just one of the many mysteries that God is unlocking for His Church.

We believe that the restoration of the anointing oil is timely and has been orchestrated by God. However, unlocking the mystery of this holy anointing oil has been controversial in some circles, because of various interpretations of Exodus 30.

In Exodus 30:25-33 we do, in-fact, read of a serious warning about the use of the holy anointing oil. Verse 33 states that *"Whoever makes perfume like it and puts it on anyone other than a priest must be cut off from their people"* (NIV). Unfortunately, this warning has separated the Church from her inheritance of the oil for numerous generations, as it has been greatly feared and misunderstood.

In David Stern's translation, *The Complete Jewish Bible*, Exodus 30:33 reads as *"Whoever makes any like it or uses it on any unauthorized person is to be cut off from his people."* A more Hebraic understanding is that *"unauthorized"* simply meant those who were not kings and priests.

It was after the rebellion of Korah (Num. 16) when God commanded the anointing oil to be set aside for priests alone. Korah and the 250 princes challenged Moses and Aaron in an attempt to overthrow their leadership. The instructions regarding the oil and its uses were consequently put in place to protect the priesthood and to prevent another rebel from duplicating the oil, and proclaiming himself as the true priest during an insurrection.

Revelation 1:6 says that "[Jesus Christ]...*has made us kings and priests to His God and Father, to Him be glory and dominion forever and ever. Amen.*" In the Greek text, "kings and priests" translates as "a kingdom of priests."

As Believers in Yeshua, Jesus, we have been called as kings and priests, and therefore, we are *authorized* to use the holy anointing oil. We are not authorized to abuse it, or to anoint man's appointments, but we are indeed called to use the oil within the Kingdom, and to anoint God's men and women—God's appointments.

We are called to be holy and set apart, and the anointing oil is simply a symbol of this separation and devotion. When you anoint your children, you are acknowledging that they belong to the Lord; when you anoint your home, you are acknowledging that your home is covered by the blood of Yeshua, Jesus, and that the culture within it reflects a Kingdom culture and not that of the world; and when you anoint the sick, you are following the instructions in James 5:14 which say:

*"Is **anyone** among you sick? Let him call for the elders of the church, and let them pray over him, anointing him with oil in the name of the Lord."* (Emphasis added)

Through the blood of Jesus, who came to fulfill the law, and our calling as kings and priests, we have been qualified to anoint with oil in the name of the Lord.

God's Anointed of the Bible

Many great heroes of the Bible were anointed with holy anointing oil. The oil was a symbol of release and spiritual recognition of calling—a consecration for the call of God on their lives.

King David

In 1 Samuel 16:1, 10-13 we read about Samuel anointing David:

"Now the LORD said to Samuel, 'How long will you mourn for Saul, seeing I have rejected him from reigning over Israel? **Fill your horn with oil, and go; I am sending you to Jesse the Bethlehemite. For I have provided Myself a king among his sons.'**

"Thus Jesse made seven of his sons pass before Samuel. And Samuel said to Jesse, 'The LORD has not chosen these.' And Samuel said to Jesse, 'Are all the young men here?' Then he said, 'There remains yet the youngest, and there he is, keeping the sheep.' And Samuel said to Jesse, 'Send and bring him. For we will not sit down till he comes here.' So he sent and brought him in. Now he

Many great heroes of the Bible were anointed with holy anointing oil.

was ruddy, with bright eyes, and good-looking. ***And the LORD said, 'Arise, anoint him; for this is the one!' Then Samuel took the horn of oil and anointed him in the midst of his brothers; and the Spirit of the LORD came upon David from that day forward…"*** (Emphasis added)

David was called out from amongst his brothers and was anointed to be King of Israel. While his kingship would not physically take place for many years, God still called on Samuel to anoint David with the holy anointing oil; this anointing set him apart for his future role as Israel's king. As it says in verse 13: *"the Spirit of the Lord came upon David **from that day forward.**"* (Emphasis added)

David was anointed to be king. He was anointed into his God-given calling and destiny. The anointing was a personal recognition of surrender to what God had preordained for David.

In 1 Chronicles 11:3 it says: *"Therefore all the elders of Israel came to the king at Hebron, and David made a covenant with them at Hebron before the LORD. And they anointed David king over Israel, according to the word of the LORD by Samuel."*

David was again anointed according to the word of the Lord spoken through the prophet several years prior. It was a physical act of honor and recognition that resulted in a spiritual activation that had both a physical and spiritual impact on David's future, and on the future of Israel.

David was again anointed according to the word of the Lord...

It was one moment, one "moed" (divine appointment), one anointing that changed history as we know it. The act of anointing is deeply and spiritually symbolic, but we *can* witness its manifestation in the natural realm.

The Disciples

In Mark 6:12-13 we read about the disciples using anointing oil after Jesus sent them out two-by-two, and after He had empowered them:

"So they went out and preached that people should repent. And they cast out many demons, and anointed with oil many who were sick, and healed them."

The anointing oil was being used by those who were *sent* and *empowered*, and was being used on those who were walking in repentance and needed a *healing touch*. The holy anointing oil was a symbolic sign of consecration and the hand of the Lord, separating man unto Himself, as if to say, "These are Mine. These are chosen. These are set apart for a purpose. These are delivered!"

In the book of Mark, we read about the anointing oil used by *empowered* disciples to heal and set free. It was a spiritual tool that they were authorized to use.

Aaron

In Leviticus 8:10-12 we read about Moses using the anointing oil to anoint Aaron for his priestly calling:

"Also Moses took the anointing oil, and anointed the tabernacle and all that was in it, and consecrated them. He sprinkled some of it on the altar seven times, anointed the altar and all its utensils, and the laver and its base, to consecrate them. And he poured some of the anointing oil on Aaron's head and anointed him, to consecrate him."

Again in Psalm 133:2-3 (NIV) we read about this anointing when David likened unity to anointing oil:

"It is like precious oil poured on the head, running down on the beard, running down on Aaron's beard, down on the collar of his robe. It is as if the dew of Hermon were falling on Mount Zion. For there the LORD bestows His blessing, even life forevermore."

The anointing oil is a symbol of separation unto God, but it is also a symbol of *unity* in the Spirit. It is a symbol of the Lord's blessing where there is life forevermore!

King Solomon

In 1 Kings 1:32-35, 39, 45 we read about a transfer of inheritance and authority when King David calls for his son, Solomon, to be anointed as King of Israel in his place. Solomon was anointed and activated as king by a priest, a prophet, and by the instruction of his father. This anointing sealed his position and his destiny:

"And King David said, 'Call to me Zadok the priest, Nathan the prophet, and Benaiah the son of Jehoiada.' So they came before the king. The king also said to them, 'Take with you the servants of your lord, and have Solomon my son ride on my own mule, and take him down to Gihon.

The anointing sealed his position and his destiny.

There let Zadok the priest and Nathan the prophet anoint him king over Israel; and blow the horn, and say, "Long live King Solomon!" Then you shall come up after him, and he shall come and sit on my throne, and he shall be king in my place. For I have appointed him to be ruler over Israel and Judah...'

"So Zadok the priest and Nathan the prophet have anointed him king at Gihon; and they have gone up from there rejoicing..."

The Priests

In Leviticus we read about the anointing oil being used to anoint the beginning of the priestly line, to separate Aaron for his calling in the Lord, and to signify the separation of Aaron's family line to be set apart to perform the priestly duties in the Temple of the Lord.

In all of these Biblical examples we see the anointing oil being used to *call out, consecrate, separate,* and to *deliver, make whole, and destroy the yoke of the enemy.*

We see the anointing oil being used by great men of faith: Samuel, Moses, and the disciples as they anointed kings, priests, prophets, and those who were sick.

Altogether the words anoint, anointing, and anointed appear nearly 300 times in the NKJV Bible. Anointing is, according to the word of God, a very important act that is given and received throughout history, as well as amongst the Body of Christ.

In short, the anointing is a sign of commissioning for position!

NOTE: If you would like to discover for yourself the biblical history of anointing oil, I encourage you to study the list of biblical references found on pages 49-51.

Part II

Part II

How the Restoration Began— A Testimony by Paul Marcellino

The restoration of the holy anointing oil began with God's hand working in many individual lives, ***including mine!*** It is something that I take very seriously and consider it a great honor to be a part of this historic restoration. I believe that unlocking the mystery of *The King's Oil* is something I have been called to be a part of since before I was in my mother's womb. As it says in Jeremiah 1:4-5:

"Then the word of the LORD came to me, saying: 'Before I formed you in the womb I knew you; before you were born I sanctified you; I ordained you a prophet to the nations.'"

We all have things in our lives that we have been called to accomplish—things we are ordained to be a part of before conception. I believe that the restoration of the holy anointing oil was something I was ordained for—something that the Lord had been preparing me for since childhood.

We all have things in our lives that we have been called to accomplish...

As a child I was blessed with a loving and supportive family. At 12 years old we were living the "American Dream" when God unexpectedly called our family to uproot and relocate to Israel.

Why Israel?

This was definitely a season of drastic change for me. In a matter of months I had gone from being home-schooled in the U.S., to attending public school in Israel, where the classes were taught only in Hebrew! Initially, I struggled with not understanding a word that was spoken. I was confused, and often wondered as I traveled the windy roads of the Galilee if my life would ever have meaning or purpose. I asked over and over: what was I doing here in Israel?

Life continued to move forward, and we settled into Israeli life and culture. After three years we returned to the United States. Even then, I wasn't sure what purpose our time in Israel had served, nor was I fully confident about the purpose that it held for my own personal life.

God Calling—A Prophetic Word

Still, life moved forward. I finished high school and began my college studies. I pursued a degree in chemistry, with a minor in biology—with plans of becoming a pharmacist. But in the midst of successful study, I slowly began to stray from my relationship with the Lord. I eventually realized that I was feeling an enormous spiritual void. I was weary of my lifestyle, but I was unsure of how to change it.

During a summer break from college I attended a Christian conference and experienced a deep encounter with the Lord—so deep that at first

I resisted. When I finally broke, I wept, I repented, and then I asked the Lord to change my heart, and vowed to follow and serve Him, and Him alone. In my desperation I asked God for a sign that He heard my cry. I didn't know how, but I wanted proof that God heard and God saw.

I soon discovered that God's response can be *very* immediate. The moment I stood up from the altar, I turned around and there, standing no more than 15 feet in front of me, was a man looking at me intently, as if he knew something that I didn't; that man was Curt Landry. We had only met briefly prior to this encounter, but this time was different. This time his eyes seemed to pierce straight through me.

Intrigued, yet slightly nervous, I walked up to him. He said that he had a word from the Lord for me, and to meet him outside in 30 minutes. I did not know at the time, but that encounter would change my life forever.

Curt prayed a very prophetic prayer over me, and everything he spoke unfolded within the next seven days. I had never experienced anything similar to this before. A word from the Lord—a word of prophecy—all of this was unfamiliar to me. However, it was like a refreshing rain in the desert. It opened my eyes and allowed me to see puzzle pieces coming together.

What was God Doing?

After a year and a half of surrendering to the Lord, I found myself involved in organizing a youth event at a conference. I invited Curt Landry's daughter, Megann, to attend as a volunteer. She had been invited twice before by other individuals, but had politely declined. However, upon receiving the third invitation she came to the realization that God was trying to get her attention, and she accepted!

Our time together at the conference marked the beginning of our lifelong relationship. Within three months we were engaged, and married nine months after that. Megann was another wonderful piece of my life's puzzle, and becoming a part of Curt and Christie Landry's family was yet another. Suddenly I found myself with many new pieces, but at the time the pieces did not seem to be connecting—I was simply collecting them.

After Megann and I had been married for a year, I prayerfully decided to turn-down my acceptance to pharmacy school. This decision presented itself as a tremendous struggle for both myself, and my family. It appeared as if my chemistry degree had been a waste of time, finances, effort, and more importantly, five years of life. At the time the pieces of my puzzle seemed scattered; my family and I were very disappointed and I was once again asking: what was God doing?

The *My Olive Tree* Vision

I was working for *House of David Ministries*, when the Lord began to open up another door for me with the birth of *My Olive Tree*. I was extremely excited about the vision of *My Olive Tree* as a vehicle to help bring the prophecies of Amos 9 and Isaiah 41 to pass—so that the desert would blossom and rejoice! As the *My Olive Tree* groves were harvested, I knew that much-needed employment would be created through the annual production of the pressed olive oil, as well as the olive oil products.

Shortly after the birth of *My Olive Tree*, the Lord began using scriptures about the olive tree and its oil to speak deep into my heart. I began to realize that our vision extended beyond the trees themselves, to the olive oil their fruit would produce.

I began studying Exodus 30 regarding the holy anointing oil recipe imparted from God to Moses. This oil, or ointment, was used to anoint, set apart and make holy that which it was applied to. My heart began to stir with the possibility of the Lord allowing *My Olive Tree* to actually be used to restore this oil. Many questions began to arise, but the most important was should we even attempt to unlock the mysteries of the oil?

I did not know that at the same time I was seeking the Lord about this restoration that the Lord was speaking to three other men of God (Curt Landry, Perry Stone, and Ron Phillips) about this very same thing—the restoration of the holy anointing oil.

Within a very short time the Lord began to confirm our vision and give us answers to our many questions. We began to diligently pray and ask the Lord to bring us *someone* who could make the anointing oil, because we read in the scripture that the oil was to be made according to the art of the biblical apothecary—or the modern-day chemist.

The End Result— *The King's Oil!*

Although I had a degree in chemistry, it never occurred to me that the chemist we were praying for would be me—that I would be the one called to physically assemble the Exodus 30 oil!

When the Lord woke me up from a deep sleep and clearly spoke that I would be the one making the holy anointing oil, I was both shocked and honored that God would call me in such a way. At the same time, I was blessed to know that once again the Lord had brought me full circle—that my studies in college were, in-fact, not a waste. My steps had been directed all along. From childhood, to my time in Israel, to studying chemistry, God had preordained my days so that I could be one of His vessels who would actually take part in the restoration of the holy anointing oil.

My Olive Tree is a vehicle to help bring the prophecies of Amos 9 and Isaiah 41 to pass.

I was about to become a part of a modern-day restoration! In Exodus 31:1-11, Bezalel was *"called by name"* and used by God to help construct the first Tent of Meeting and make the sacred anointing oil. God also specifically called Zerubbabel to rebuild the Temple (Ezra 3, Hag., Zech. 4:6-10). As was then, I believe that today the Lord is once again calling many modern-day Bezalel's and Zerubbabel's to restore the Tabernacle of David as it was prophesied in Amos 9:11.

Within a few short years it seemed that the pieces of my life's puzzle were beginning to fit together to form a vision. We continued to spend many hours in prayer and study, trusting in the Lord to reveal to us exactly how to make the oil according to the biblical instructions. We sought the revelation of the Lord in this matter, and step-by-step He guided our hands and our minds until we had the end result—*The King's Oil!*

Part III

Part III

The Restoration of *The King's Oil!*

When we embrace prophecy, we are better able to understand how God is moving around us. The restoration of *The King's Oil* is truly about prophecy fulfilled—about unlocking the mysteries that have been denied to the Church for centuries. It is a sign of the times and the season that we live in; a season when God is actively working through us, His Church, to reveal His mysteries—mysteries that have been concealed since the early Church met at Elvira and Nicaea in the 3rd century!

The return of the biblical anointing oil is a physical sign of the spiritual manifestation of *The King's Oil* returning to the earth. It is a sign of the coming manifestation of God's glory and the anointing for both king and priest. This anointing of king and priest represents Godly order as seen in the five-fold ministry, and sets the stage for God to work among us.

The oil is a sign of that which is to come.

In biblical times the sanctuary and the utensils would have been anointed in the Temple. The king and the priest would have also been anointed. This anointing represented a spiritual commissioning and a divine right of dominion. As mentioned earlier, we have been called to be as priests (Rev. 1:6), and the physical act of anointing is simply a reflection of the spiritual call and authority given to us by the Lord—a symbol that the "yoke" of the enemy has been broken over our lives.

In Hebrew, the word holy, as in "holy anointing oil," is *"kadosh"* which means to be separated. As Believers, we have been called to be separated unto the Lord. When we are anointed, it is as a symbol to the world that the Lord has set us apart for His good works. In essence, as if the Lord marked us and said, *"he or she is mine."* We have been separated for empowerment and preparation!

The oil is a sign of that which is to come. It is also a sign of sanctification and a prophetic sign that holiness, not in religious legalism, but in revelation, is finally being restored to the Church. The Lord wants to sanctify our lives, our homes, our finances, and our churches.

For the most part, our society does not understand separation—but God is restoring this back to His people. The blood of Jesus has separated us from the world and we are being called to walk this out. This is a calling. This is a lifestyle!

Yeshua—The Anointed One

When we are physically anointed it represents a spiritual authorization to serve God in an area of honor or responsibility, just as it was for the kings, priests, and prophets. This anointing also represents a Divine calling or enabling to carry out these positions and responsibilities. As we see in many biblical ceremonies it represents part of the process of induction into leadership and empowerment.

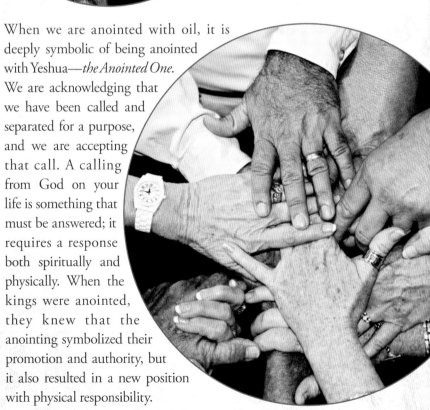

Many Believers have been anointed, but Yeshua, Jesus, was literally "The Anointed One." The transliteration of the Hebrew term, *Mashiach* is Messiah, or as seen in the Greek, *Christos*. Both Messiah and *Christos* mean "The Anointed One." The verb *"mashach"* is the root word of *Mashiach* and is seen in the Old Testament nearly 140 times, alternately translated as "to smear, anoint, or spread."

When we are anointed with oil, it is deeply symbolic of being anointed with Yeshua—*the Anointed One.* We are acknowledging that we have been called and separated for a purpose, and we are accepting that call. A calling from God on your life is something that must be answered; it requires a response both spiritually and physically. When the kings were anointed, they knew that the anointing symbolized their promotion and authority, but it also resulted in a new position with physical responsibility.

You Are the Temple of God

Being anointed represents an acknowledgment of surrender. When the priests were anointed they were accepting their call into the priesthood, which would impact their lives in every way. They *became* their calling, and being a priest became their identity; their priesthood was not a Monday through Friday job with weekends free to be lived how they chose. They were called and anointed to be priests—all day, every day. They were surrendered. They were free from the yoke of the enemy. When we truly surrender *we relinquish control—we abandon our rights.*

The anointing, together with the call, is not always convenient, and is certainly not comfortable. It is demanding and requires us to abandon our rights; living lives of surrender.

*"Do you not know that **you are the temple** of God and that the Spirit of God dwells in you?"*—1 Corinthians 3:16 (Emphasis added)

You are the temple of God! Which means that you were made to be a habitation for His Spirit. You were called to be holy, sanctified, and set-apart; and you were called to be free.

Your Anointing—Kingdom Property

When we anoint our homes and our businesses we are declaring that these areas are being called forth to serve and prosper with a Kingdom purpose—just as when the utensils of the Temple were anointed to be used in worship. We are declaring that our homes, our assets, our finances, our gifts, our talents, our abilities—all the things that are under our authority—are protected and have been set apart to freely serve the King and to prosper the Kingdom.

It is important for us to remember that our callings and anointing belong to the Lord and His Kingdom. You may be blessed and you may prosper—that is God's heart for you. However, your anointing belongs to Him and was not given for personal worldly promotion;

your anointing was given to be a blessing in God's Kingdom. Thus, your anointing must be surrendered to the Lord.

The anointing on your life is God's chosen gift for you. Samuel passed by many of David's brothers, but the kingship was clearly reserved for David alone. God called David out from among them. We do not get to choose our calling—God chooses it for us. But we do have a free will to make choices that will either positively or negatively impact our lives for what God has for us.

1 Corinthians 6:19 says, *"Or do you not know that your body is the temple of the Holy Spirit who is in you, whom you have from God, and **you are not your own?"*** (Emphasis added)

Callings and anointing must be tended to. They require food, water, and protection in order to grow. When you are physically anointed it is a symbolic act, but it requires physical attention. The anointing process is just the first step to unlocking the life of the calling that awaits. It awaits your obedience for steps two, three, four, and onward.

Sanctified and Set Apart

The Lord has called His Bride to be obedient and sanctified. When one is sanctified

> The anointing on your life is God's chosen gift for you.

they are *set apart* for sacred use, or *purified*. The dictionary describes sanctification as *"a religious ceremony where something is made holy."* As Believers, we have been sanctified; we have been made holy through the blood of Yeshua, Jesus. The Messiah, the Anointed One, has separated us unto Himself to fulfill the calling He has placed upon our lives. When we are anointed, it is simply a physical demonstration of our recognition of His calling and our need for activation and separation.

Unlocking the Mysteries of *The King's Oil!*

With all that said about anointing, perhaps you are still asking, *"why specifically The King's Oil?"* The King's Oil is not a magic formula. It is simply different, and prophetically speaks of the season we are living in. For many years the Church has been removed from the roots of our faith, and now we are witnessing a revival of interest in unlocking the mysteries of the Jewish roots of the Christian faith. We are stepping back and connecting with our roots. We are following the instructions left to us in Exodus 30 and activating the promises for this generation.

Exodus 30:31 says, *"And you shall speak to the children of Israel, saying: 'This shall be a holy anointing oil to Me **throughout your generations**.'"* (Emphasis added)

We believe that the anointing oil of Exodus 30 is a blessing of our spiritual inheritance that was not just for our ancestors, but for this generation too!

"This shall be a holy anointing oil to Me throughout your generations."

-Exodus 30:31

It is our prayer that after reading this booklet you will have a better understanding of the physical restoration of *The King's Oil*, and will feel confident to use it as a spiritual tool. It has been prophesied that this oil will be used around the world and therefore, it is our hope that through a better understanding of *The King's Oil* you will be inspired to carry it to the nations and help unlock its mysteries for Believers everywhere.

The anointing oil is a spiritual tool that the Lord gave to His people, and now we are witnessing a return of this oil with its original instructions and components. We would encourage you to use *The King's Oil* to pray for your families, to separate your homes, to pray for the sick, and to destroy the yoke—the burdens of the enemy.

"It shall come to pass in that day that his burden will be taken away from your shoulder, and his yoke from your neck, and the yoke will be destroyed because of the anointing oil."—Isaiah 10:27

Biblical References

Desert
Isaiah 32:15
Isaiah 43:20

Garden
Ezekiel 36:35
Amos 9:14

Negev
Joshua 15:19
Judges 1:15
Jeremiah 32:44

Oil
Genesis 28:18
Genesis 35:14
Exodus 25:6
Exodus 27:20
Exodus 29:2
Exodus 29:7
Exodus 29:21
Exodus 29:23
Exodus 29:40
Exodus 30:24-25
Exodus 30:31
Exodus 31:11
Exodus 35:8
Exodus 35:14-15
Exodus 35:28
Exodus 37:29
Exodus 39:37-38
Exodus 40:9
Leviticus 2:1-7
Leviticus 2:15-16
Leviticus 5:11
Leviticus 6:15

Leviticus 6:21
Leviticus 7:10
Leviticus 7:12
Leviticus 8:2
Leviticus 8:10
Leviticus 8:12
Leviticus 8:26
Leviticus 8:30
Leviticus 9:4
Leviticus 10:7
Leviticus 14:10
Leviticus 14:12
Leviticus 14:15-18
Leviticus 14:21
Leviticus 14:24
Leviticus 14:26-29
Leviticus 21:10
Leviticus 21:12
Leviticus 23:13
Leviticus 24:2
Numbers 4:9
Numbers 4:16
Numbers 5:15
Numbers 6:15
Numbers 7:13
Numbers 7:19
Numbers 7:25
Numbers 7:31
Numbers 7:37
Numbers 7:43
Numbers 7:49
Numbers 7:55
Numbers 7:61
Numbers 7:67
Numbers 7:73

Numbers 7:79
Numbers 8:8
Numbers 11:8
Numbers 15:4
Numbers 15:6
Numbers 15:9
Numbers 18:12
Numbers 28:5
Numbers 28:9
Numbers 28:12-13
Numbers 28:20
Numbers 28:28
Numbers 29:3
Numbers 29:9
Numbers 29:14
Numbers 35:25
Deuteronomy 7:13
Deuteronomy 8:8
Deuteronomy 11:14
Deuteronomy 12:17
Deuteronomy 14:23
Deuteronomy 18:4
Deuteronomy 28:40
Deuteronomy 28:51
Deuteronomy 32:13
Deuteronomy 33:24
1 Samuel 10:1
1 Samuel 16:1
1 Samuel 16:13
2 Samuel 1:21
2 Samuel 14:2
1 Kings 1:39
1 Kings 5:11
1 Kings 17:12

Oil (cont.)

1 Kings 17:14
1 Kings 17:16
2 Kings 4:2
2 Kings 4:6-7
2 Kings 9:1
2 Kings 9:3
2 Kings 9:6
2 Kings 18:32
1 Chronicles 9:29
1 Chronicles 12:40
1 Chronicles 27:28
2 Chronicles 2:10
2 Chronicles 2:15
2 Chronicles 11:11
2 Chronicles 31:5
2 Chronicles 32:28
Ezra 3:7
Ezra 6:9
Ezra 7:22
Nehemiah 5:11
Nehemiah 10:37
Nehemiah 10:39
Nehemiah 13:5
Nehemiah 13:12
Esther 2:12
Job 24:11
Job 29:6
Psalm 23:5
Psalm 45:7
Psalm 89:20
Psalm 92:10
Psalm 104:15
Psalm 109:18
Psalm 141:5
Proverbs 21:20

Isaiah 41:19
Isaiah 61:3
Jeremiah 31:12
Jeremiah 40:10
Jeremiah 41:8
Ezekiel 16:9
Ezekiel 16:13
Ezekiel 16:18-19
Ezekiel 23:41
Ezekiel 27:17
Ezekiel 32:14
Ezekiel 45:14
Ezekiel 45:24-25
Ezekiel 46:5
Ezekiel 46:7
Ezekiel 46:11
Ezekiel 46:14-15
Hosea 2:5
Hosea 2:22
Hosea 12:1
Joel 1:10
Joel 2:19
Joel 2:24
Micah 6:7
Micah 6:15
Haggai 1:11
Haggai 2:12
Zechariah 4:12
Matthew 25:3-4
Matthew 25:8
Mark 6:13
Luke 7:46
Luke 10:34
Luke 16:6
Hebrews 1:9

James 5:14
Revelation 6:6
Revelation 18:13

Olive / Olive Trees

Genesis 8:11
Exodus 23:11
Exodus 27:20
Exodus 30:24
Leviticus 24:2
Deuteronomy 6:11
Deuteronomy 8:8
Deuteronomy 24:20
Deuteronomy 28:40
Judges 9:8-9
Judges 15:5
1 Kings 6:23
1 Kings 6:31-33
1 Chronicles 27:28
Nehemiah 8:15
Psalm 52:8
Psalm 128:3
Isaiah 17:6
Isaiah 24:13
Jeremiah 11:16
Hosea 14:6
Amos 4:9
Micah 6:15
Habakkuk 3:17
Haggai 2:19
Zechariah 4:3
Zechariah 4:11-12
Zechariah 14:4
Matthew 21:1
Matthew 24:3

Olive / Olive Trees (cont.)
Matthew 26:30
Mark 11:1
Mark 13:3
Mark 14:26
Luke 19:29
Luke 19:37
Luke 21:37
Luke 22:39
John 8:1
Acts 1:12
Romans 11:17
Romans 11:24
James 3:12
Revelation 11:4

Olive Grove
Deuteronomy 6:11
Joshua 24:13
1 Samuel 8:14
2 Kings 5:26
2 Kings 18:32
Nehemiah 5:11
Nehemiah 9:25
Isaiah 41:17-20
Haggai 2:19

Springs / Water
Exodus 15:27
Deuteronomy 8:7
Joshua 15:19
Joshua 16:1
Psalm 107:35
Isaiah 35:1
Isaiah 35:6-7

Holy Anointing Oil (Exodus 30)

1/2 ounce
glass bottle

Price: $10.00 USD
plus S&H

Made in accordance with Exodus 30, *My Olive Tree* is excited to offer *The King's Oil-Holy Anointing Oil!*

Using ancient apothecary methods, *The King's Oil-Holy Anointing Oil* carries a unique aroma, texture and color inherent in its Biblical root ingredients. Produced exclusively by *My Olive Tree*, *The King's Oil-Holy Anointing Oil* uses only the finest ingredients, including oil harvested by *My Olive Tree* in the land of Israel!

Break the Yoke Today
When You Order *The King's Oil-Holy Anointing Oil!*
please visit www.CurtLandry.com/store or call 1.800.334.3132

Take covenant root in the Nation of Israel by sponsoring an olive tree with **MY OLIVE TREE.**

THANK YOU FOR PLANTING INTO ISRAEL'S FUTURE!

Sponsor an olive tree today and MY OLIVE TREE will send you a one-half ounce bottle of *The King's Oil—Holy Anointing Oil,* along with your "Certificate of Authenticity" in your name or the name of a loved one to commemorate your sponsorship. This certificate is suitable for framing and can be displayed as a testimony of your love and support of the Nation of Israel!

PLACE YOUR ORDER TODAY!

Call: 800.334.3132 or Email: info@myolivetree.com
My Olive Tree, P.O. Box 193, Fairland, OK 74343

For more information about the MY OLIVE TREE project please visit: www.myolivetree.com/video

PLANT INTO THE FUTURE OF ISRAEL TODAY!

Your heartfelt generosity will give life, support families and children, and build Israel's economy. Join us as we plant, harvest, and cause the desert to bloom!

Holy Anointing Oil (Exodus 30)

Now Available in 16 pack!

Made in accordance with Exodus 30, *My Olive Tree* is excited to offer *The King's Oil-Holy Anointing Oil* at a discounted price in 16 pack quantities! And, as an added bonus, you will receive a beautiful point-of-purchase display at no extra cost.

For special wholesale pricing and to place your order please call 1.800.334.3132

PROVIDING SAFEHOUSES FOR YOUNG ADULTS

M COVENANT PARTNERS BLESSING HOLOCAUST SURVIVORS.

EERS DISTRIBUTE FOOD TO NEEDY MILITARY FAMILIES.

A Veritas Entertainment Film

ILLUMINATIONS

One New MAN, One New LIFE

AN EXTRAORDINARY BIBLICAL SERIES
FILMED ON LOCATION IN THE LAND OF ISRAEL
Hosted by Curt Landry

1-800-334-3132
www.MyOliveTree.com/Illuminations

DEAD SEA MORINGA

A Natural Source of Vitamins & Minerals!

One of Nature's best-kept Secrets! Moringa is considered by many as the most nutrient rich plant food source found on earth, naturally containing 90 Nutrients, including 12 Vitamins and Minerals, 46 Antioxidants, 18 Amino Acids, including a high concentration of all 9 Essential Amino Acids.

Dead Sea—MORINGA is grown in the southern region of Israel near the Dead Sea where the Moringa plant thrives. Dead Sea—MORINGA produces significantly higher levels of vitamin E and Omega 3, 6, and 9 when compared with traditionally grown Moringa. Today, the Dead Sea boasts over 1 million visitors every year—most of whom have come to soak in the Dead Sea's healing waters and take advantage of the health benefits associated with the Dead Sea's natural mineral-infused water and mud.

When compared to other key sources of nutrients, gram for gram, Dead Sea—MORINGA contains:

• 7 times the vitamin C of oranges
• 3 times the iron of spinach
• 4 times the calcium of milk
• 4 times the vitamin A of carrots
• 2 times the protein of milk
• 3 times the potassium of bananas
• 3 times the vitamin E of almonds

Moringa has been used for thousands of years as a naturally occurring supplement. Moringa's various components provide it with unusual nutritional value, promoting overall health and wellness. Moringa helps maintain joints, the immune system and appetite in children and adults, as well as being a good source of vitamin E and Omega 3.

Price: $39.95 plus S&H
120 Vegetarian Capsule Bottle

DEAD SEA MORINGA™

For Best Results! Take 1-2 **Dead Sea—MORINGA** capsules, 2 times per day before meals.

Note: Due to a lifetime of diets lacking in minerals and nutrients, along with the stress that ailments can create on the body, we recommend allowing 90 days to begin noticing results from use of **Dead Sea—MORINGA**. Our bodies take time to heal and respond to the many benefits that **Dead Sea—MORINGA** can provide.

der Dead Sea—MORINGA at www.DeadSeaMoringa.com or call 1.855.208.6302

About the Author

Curt & Christie Landry

Curt Landry is the founder and CEO of *Curt Landry Ministries*, an apostle and founder of *House of David Ministries*, and the acting CEO of *My Olive Tree*. Curt and his wife Christie travel extensively operating in the gifts of healing, signs and wonders, and teaching about the Jewish roots of the Christian faith and the *One New Man*. Curt is also active in raising support for Israel throughout the Evangelical community as he desires to be a bridge of unity and restoration between Israel and the Church.

About the Author

Paul & Megann Marcellino

Paul and Megann Marcellino are the organizational force behind *Curt Landry Ministries*, *My Olive Tree*, and *House of David Ministries*. They serve beside Curt and Christie Landry, and are blessed to help support the God-given vision of all three organizations. God has called Paul and Megann to be an active voice for the *One New Man*, having a heart to bless the Church, Israel and the nations. Together, and as part of the Landry family, they are raising support and awareness of the *One New Man*—bringing the Kingdom to the nations.